Evening **Express**

ABERDEEN
IN THE SEVENTIES
A Decade of Change

RAYMOND ANDERSON

breedon **books**
PUBLISHING

First published in Great Britain in 2003 by
The Breedon Books Publishing Company Limited
Breedon House, 3 The Parker Centre,
Derby, DE21 4SZ.

ISBN 1 85983 372 1

Printed and bound by Butler & Tanner,
Frome, Somerset, England.

Cover printing by Lawrence-Allen Colour Printers,
Weston-super-Mare, Somerset, England.

ABERDEEN
IN THE SEVENTIES
A Decade of Change

Contents

Acknowledgements

AS ever I have a number of people to thank for helping to get this book to the publishers.

Special thanks to Duncan Smith of the *Evening Express* library whose constant good humour when dealing with my many requests and queries was a greater tribute to his patience than my forbearance. Bob Stewart was also a big help in my researches.

The fifth book in this series covers a decade which had more source material than the other four books could rely on, making the process of selection that much more demanding.

Bruce Irvine of our photography department unearthed some of the best images, going through old files and tracing and printing pictures which have been unseen for decades, and in some cases have never been published before.

In compiling these books I am always keenly aware of the professionalism of the *Aberdeen Journals* staff photographers who took so many of them. Men like the late Ian Hardie who through their daily work have created such a rich record of life in the North-east of Scotland.

Other photographers we owe a debt to are Gordon Bissett, Charlie Flett, Jack Cryle, David Sutherland, Jim Love, Donald Stewart and many others who have served their local populations so well over the years.

As ever in these projects I relied on Susan McKay of the *Aberdeen Journals* retail unit to help smooth the bumpy road from idea to final product.

Thanks also to my wife, Arlyn, who always knew when things were going well – or not so well – with the book.

Introduction

THE past is a foreign country. They do things differently there, wrote the novelist L.P. Hartley.

After sifting through hundreds of old pictures for this book on the north-east of Scotland in the 1970s I'm bound to agree with that view.

Although I had not considered that decade 'old' enough when I compiled the first of the five books in this series in 1994 my opinion has changed. I'm sure that brash, confident 10 years are now ready for the nostalgia treatment.

The Seventies have certainly improved with age. Those of us who had lived our youth in the Sixties regarded the following decade as distinctly un-cool. But was it really the age that taste forgot? There's plenty of evidence to support that view. Kipper ties, bell-bottom trousers, tank-tops, glitter make-up, platform-sole shoes. It was a time of excess.

However, there was much that stood the test of time. For instance the best of the television programmes, movies and books. In the Seventies we could settle down in front of our three-channel televisions and watch classic comedies like *Fawlty Towers*, *Porridge* and *The Goodies*, as well as ground-breaking series like *The Sweeney*. Then there were the superheroes of the Seventies. *The Six Million Dollar Man* and *Wonderwoman* were two favourites that kept children in front of the television screens of the North-east.

Not that we got all our pop culture from the small screen. Hugely influential pop artists found their way to Aberdeen. Led Zeppelin and David Bowie honed their acts before Aberdeen audiences in the Seventies.

The multi-screen cinema was still a long way off but many of the movies were impressive enough to fill the biggest of our cinema houses. *Jaws*, *Star Wars*, *The Godfather*, *Rocky*, *Clockwork Orange*, *Taxi Driver*, *One Flew Over The Cuckoo's Nest* are evidence that the decade hit a rich seam of directorial and acting talent.

Books that were in big demand at our libraries in the Seventies included Alex Haley's *Roots* which made family history a favoured pastime, *Watership Down*, which had us crying over Bright Eyes, and *The Female Eunuch* which brought bright young Australian academic Germaine Greer to public notice.

And on stage in 1973 the 7:84 Theatre Company of Scotland and their dynamic artistic director, John McGrath, got themselves noticed with *The Cheviot, The Stag* and the *Black, Black Oil*.

For the north-east of Scotland the black, black oil had been having an impact from the very dawn of the decade. By June 1970 brief reports in the local Press of oil company interest in the North Sea had grown into talk of multi-million pound exploration. But it was a few years before the cautious folk of the north-east accepted they really were at the epicentre of a remarkable industrial operation that was pushing back the frontiers of technology and engineering. The oil revolution brought considerable wealth and job opportunities to the area, but in time there would also be the Piper Alpha tragedy.

In this compilation you can see that much of the story of Aberdeen in the Seventies sprang from that discovery of oil in the North Sea. There's the huge changes at the harbour and the airport, the demolition of old parts of the city and the rapid spread of new building, including the new suburbs.

It would, however, be wrong to suggest that oil dominates this book. The folk of Aberdeen and the north-east are still the focal point. Laughing at adversity, staying true to old ways, adapting to new ways, but most of all having fun. You'll find a lot of smiles on the pages that follow.

So enjoy this snapshot of the way we lived then... when we did things a little bit differently.

Raymond Anderson
Aberdeen
Summer 2003

Protest on the March

Conservative Society students at Aberdeen University stage a protest when a busload of Russian students arrived at the Students' Union for a dinner given by the Students' Representative Council in February 1970. A Conservative Society member said: 'It is too often forgotten that the USSR are practising a harsh, repressive and intolerant regime.' An SRC spokesman condemned the demonstrators as 'puerile'.

The Russian visitors who attended a civic reception at Aberdeen Town House in 1970 walk past protesters.

A one-hour strike which was staged by the staff of an Aberdeen assurance company in 1970 in support of a claim for union recognition.

Viscount Stonehaven and Tory MP Alick Buchanan-Smith (left), talk to protesting farmers outside Mackie Academy in 1970. The demonstration was staged to let Lord Hughes, Minister of State for Scotland, know the strength of their feelings during a visit to the academy. A petition on farm prices and rewards was handed over and the quiet demonstration dispersed.

The Tory industrial relations legislation brings protesters out on to Union Street, Aberdeen, as they march to the Music Hall for a rally in 1971.

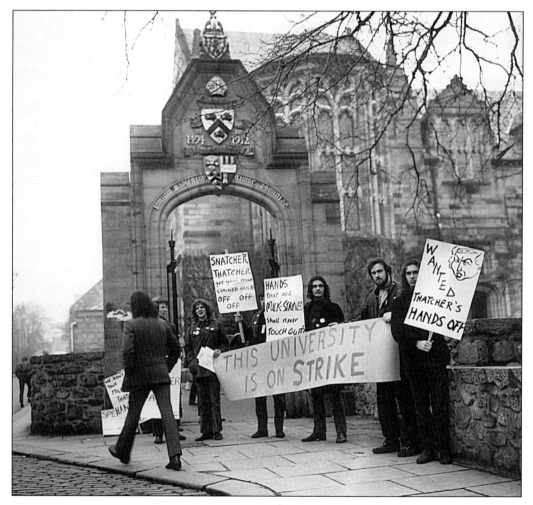

Aberdeen University student pickets at King's College in 1971. Margaret Thatcher's scrapping of free milk is the target of this protest.

Councillor Alex Collie smiles through a protest outside Aberdeen Town House in 1972.

Aberdeen building trade workers on the march in Union Street, Aberdeen, in 1972 as they head for Queen's Links for a mass meeting.

Some of the 500 Aberdeen hospital workers who marched along Union Street as part of a nationwide protest over pay in 1972.

Hundreds of protesters wend their way from the quadrangle at Marischal College in a 1973 march against the level of student grants.

Some of the College of Commerce protesters on the march over student grants in 1973.

May Day marchers on their way to a rally at the Kingsway, Aberdeen, in 1973.

Dispute over. A smiling 'clippie' at Guild Street bus station is glad to be back at work in 1974 after a dispute was settled and picketing ended.

Teachers disillusioned over pay marched along Union Street, Aberdeen, in 1974 with banners raised. Some pupils, happy to have a day off school, joined in.

Demonstrators dressed as a bride, a prostitute, a pregnant woman, a student and a housewife make their point outside the Music Hall, Aberdeen, in 1975. The protesters, outside an exhibition to mark International Women's Year, claimed it fostered the traditional image of woman as cook, housekeeper and general dogsbody in the home.

MIS-USED

MIS-LAID

MIS-CONCEIVED

Who is representing
Women's Liberation Groups?
National Abortion Campaign?
Lesbians? Prostitutes?
Battered Wives?
THIS EXHIBITION IS A FARCE

Some of the protesters at Woodhill House, Aberdeen, in 1976 to hand a petition in to Grampian Regional Council complaining about proposed increases in fees for use of community centres.

Students who staged a sit-in at Aberdeen College of Education in May 1976 in protest at Government plans to prune £57million from the Scottish Education budget by 1980. All Scotland's teacher training colleges were occupied in this concerted effort to change a deeply unpopular Tory policy.

Student protesters listen to Stanley Allan, vice-chairman of Aberdeen Trades Council, outside Woodhill House in May 1976 as the weeks-long College of Education protest sit-in continued.

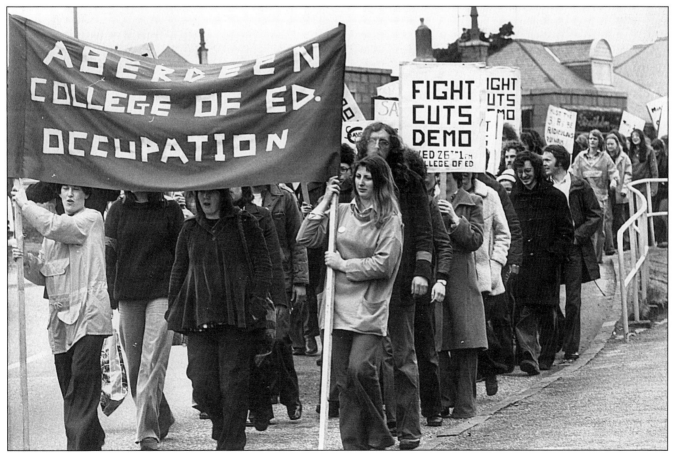

Aberdeen College of Education students marching to a rally at Grampian Regional Council's Woodhill House in support of the College of Education sit-in.

Students, many of them supporters of the Zimbabwe ZIPA nationalist movement, gather to greet Robert Blackwell, a former US State Department official, who addressed the Political Studies Society at Aberdeen University. Mr Blackwell told the protesters that Rhodesian leader Ian Smith only accepted the necessity of majority rule after pressure from US Secretary of State Dr Henry Kissinger's shuttle-diplomacy.

It's November 25, 1976 and students from Aberdeen College of Education are demonstrating outside Grampian Regional Council headquarters in support of an increase in student association fees to pay for a sabbatical for student presidents.

A 1976 student and trade unionist march in protest at Government cuts in public spending and high unemployment.

Some of the 300 Aberdeen University students who took over the Administration Building on October 20, 1977. The protest was over the university's refusal to sell shares in companies with South African dealings. At an earlier meeting nearly 700 students agreed to politely ask the administrative staff to leave the building.

A member of Aberdeen University staff picks his way through the crowded corridors of the Administration Building in 1977.

Students marching down Union Street for a rally at the Music Hall in 1977 protesting over Government cuts in education.

More public spending cuts protests in 1977. These are members of NUPE, the public employee's union, and the local government worker's union, NALGO.

About 300 demonstrators, including a large contingent of students, marching along a wet Union Street in 1977 on a 'day of action' over public spending cuts.

Grampian Regional councillor William Rose talks to pickets outside Woodhill House in November 1977. Councillors had to run a gauntlet of two sets of pickets. One group were protesting over a lack of day-care nurseries for single parents and firemen were trying to get councillors to back their wage claim..

Woodhill House is again the target of protesters in this picture. This is 1977 and demonstrators line the entrance to the HQ of Grampian Regional Council. This double protest was over a lack of Community Centre facilities in Torry, Aberdeen, and a closure-threatened nursery.

The target of these demonstrators in 1978 was the film *The Wild Geese*. They claimed the star-studded film about white mercenaries rescuing a deposed president of a southern African was 'racist-inspired propaganda'.

Aberdeen students picket Barclays Bank on Union Street in 1978 because of the company's links with South Africa.

A march along Union Street in 1978 bringing attention to the high levels of unemployment. Leading the way to an Aberdeen Trades Council rally in the Music Hall are Eric Clarke, general secretary of the National Union of Mineworkers, Jimmy Milne, general secretary of the STUC and Ron Webster of the Trades Council.

In September 1978, Prince Charles visited Aberdeen and a few protesters among the crowds raised placards opposed to British troops in Ulster.

Striking members of the sheriff clerk's department in Aberdeen picket the Sheriff Court during a civil servants' pay dispute in 1979.

A protest march by 1,200 students calling on the Government to abandon plans to increase the fees of overseas students. This event in Aberdeen on November 7, 1979, was part of a week of action organised countrywide by the National Union of Students.

Torchlit march by 200 women protesting about rape
moves along Union Street in 1979.

Women on the Saturday night
Reclaim the Night torchlit
protest march shout out their
message at the Music Hall.

Oil and Gas

The Queen officially starts the oil flowing from the Forties Field at an historic occasion at the BP complex, Dyce, in 1975.

The scene at the Forties Field switch-on ceremony when the Queen addressed the audience in 1975.

A royal hello from Aberdeen as the Queen goes walkabout among the crowds at Dyce on the day she set the oil flowing from the Forties Field.

The year is 1979 and oil company headquarters are springing up in Aberdeen. Here the new Prime MInister, Margaret Thatcher, is opening the Shell-Expro operations centre at Altens.

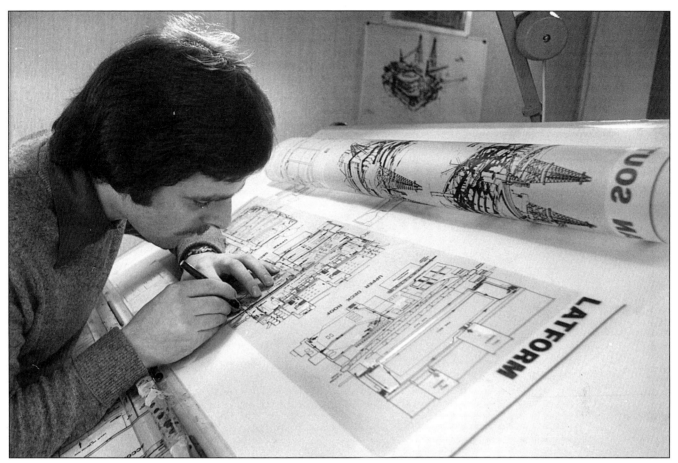

Draughtsman Neil Donald hard at work on an oil platform drawing at Chevron's Caledonian House, Aberdeen, in 1978.

Production supervisor Sandy Findlay explains a section of the Ninian Southern platform to trainee operators at the Chevron training centre in Aberdeen.

Technical assistant Lynn Milne points to where the
Chevron (UK) efforts are concentrated at the Ninian
Field. Looking on in this picture from 1978 are (from
left) Wilford Lee, general engineering, and Dick
Stephen of production engineering.

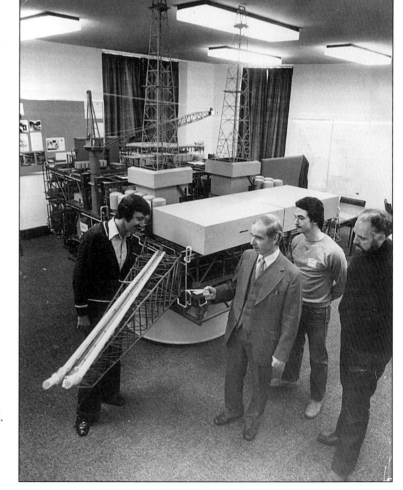

A model of the Ninian Central platform is put to use
in the operators' training centre in Aberdeen in 1978.
Here training co-ordinator Sam Alexander uses the
model to illustrate some points about the flare
boom.

Aberdeen Lord Provost William Fraser is shown the shape of Ninian House which was being built for the Chevron oil company at Altens in 1978. General manager Charles Blomberg is pointing out one of the features of the futuristic building.

The architects' ideas take form as Ninian House is built at the Altens estate in 1979.

The £450,000 Aberdeen
supply base for Chevron's
Southern platform of their
Ninian oil field at Matthew's
Quay in 1978.

The Offshore Europe exhibition hall at Bridge of Don in 1977 was the largest of its kind in the world. It was designed as a building with a life of up to 25 years by Orbits Structures, a member of the Aberdeen-based Aberglen Holdings group of companies. The complete hall was erected in under a month by only 16 men. In the early days of the exhibition when Offshore Scotland 1973 came to Aberdeen the demand for accommodation was so great it was virtually impossible to get a hotel room in or around the city. Bigger aircraft were put on the Aberdeen routes to cope with the extra passengers.

An oil rig supply ship ploughing through North Sea waves off Aberdeen in December 1978.

Meeting the immense challenge of taking oil from below the North Sea. The 23,000-ton steel jacket Highland One is secured to the seabed on the Forties Field by the giant crane barges Hercules and Thor in 1974. The jacket was for the BP platform Forties Charlie and was placed in 416ft of water. The jacket – the lower section of the platform which is fixed to the seabed – had been towed 200 miles from the Highlands Fabricators yard on the Cromarty Firth at Nigg. After pile hammers drove the 12 piles to a depth of 260ft a temporary deck was placed on the platform while further pile-driving took place during the winter.

An Aberdeen group all set to fly off to Texas for the Houston oil exhibition in 1975.

An oil rig or platform lifeboat is tested at Aberdeen Harbour in 1975.

The first woman on the offshore survival course takes the plunge at Robert Gordon Institute of Technology in Aberdeen. The year is 1977 and the woman is Dorinda Kelly.

A reassuring wave from Dorinda Kelly on the RGIT offshore survival course.

Personnel officer Carol McKay of Aberdeen posed a problem for an Occidental offshore installation manager when fog rolled in and stranded her offshore in August 1979. There were no sleeping facilities on the all-male platform, but the manager moved out of his cabin and Carol, 28, became the first woman to spend the night aboard one of Occidental's North Sea installations. She received a certificate proclaiming her as the 'first woman sleeper'.

The old gas is 'flared off' in Summerhill in 1977 to make way for gas from the southern North Sea fields. The flaring cleared out the redundant manufactured gas.

An armful of ration books for north-east drivers in the Aberdeen General Post Office strongroom in 1973. From the left are John Shepherd, assistant head postmaster; overseer Adam Smart and postal assistant Leonora Montgomery. The Government cut Britain's fuel supply by 10% and put a 50mph restriction on all non-motorway roads. By the end of November the precautionary issuing of ration books began. It was not until May 1974 that the curbs on petrol supplies to garages were lifted.

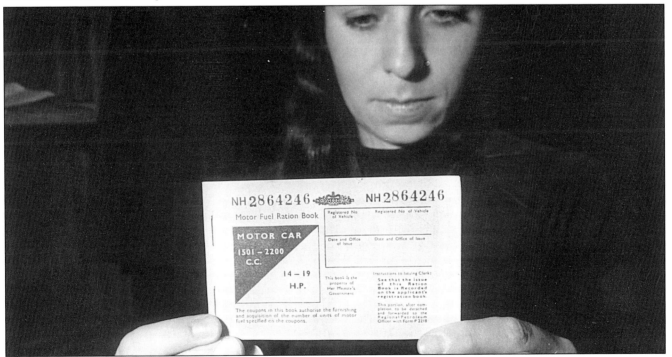

Our reliance on fuel was brought home to everyone in November 1973 when petrol rationing was a possibility and Aberdeen's Head Post Office had to plan for the distribution of 96,245 petrol ration books to 250 offices in Aberdeenshire, Banff and Kincardine. Arab-Israeli tensions and war had brought a cut in supplies of oil to Britain by 15% causing queues for petrol and the issuing of ration books.

Gateway to the North Sea

In 1971 Clydebank shipyard workers defied the Government's attempt to put Upper Clyde Shipbuilders into liquidation. Here Gerry Ross, convener of the UCS shop stewards, addresses workers from an improvised stage in the plating shed at the John

Lewis yard. Standing on a four-foot high stack of sheet metal he told the Aberdeen men: 'The Clydeside workers are not kidding when we say to the Government "you are not on".' To help the workers in their fight with the Government men from Hall Russell, John Lewis and other smaller Aberdeen yards pledged financial support to the workers in their struggle, which was eventually successful.

The biggest vessel to come from Aberdeen's Hall Russell yard by 1971 was this 10,500-ton cargo ship being built for Dutch owners. In this picture a welder is at work on the bow of the ship as it projects over a street beside the yard.

In 1973 Aberdeen Harbour is showing signs of overcrowding with double parking of cargo vessels waiting to be discharged on top of the normal harbour traffic.

The oil rig supply ship which the Hall Russell yard sold for almost £1million under construction on the left of this picture from March 1973. Stretching across the centre background of the picture are the excavations for a new £600,000 graving dock.

By September 1973 this was the face of Footdee with the driving in of sheet piling well advanced for the new graving dock at Hall Russell's yard. The new drydock was to be completed to coincide with the Harbour Board's conversion of the Victoria and Upper docks into a tidal harbour.

In July 1974 the new giant graving dock nears completion at the Footdee yard of Hall Russell. This picture was taken from York Street looking across the Dee to Torry.

The new graving dock at Hall Russell in use in 1975 with an oil-rig supply ship undergoing repair. The dock at 370ft long and 70ft wide was a the largest on the east coast, north of the Tyne.

The 'control tower' of Aberdeen Harbour where a new surveillance radar system came into operation in November 1974. Round House attendant John Dey is contacting a Polish trawler entering the harbour while navigation control officer Captain Frederick Tait stands by the radar which was helping to control the ever-increasing traffic at the port.

Aberdeen's bustling harbour with the new dry docks to the fore in 1974.

The build up of offshore traffic didn't cause Aberdeen's traditional port industry to be forgotten. Here a new mechanical lift for loading and unloading trawlers is demonstrated in 1974

The little ships blockade ends after three days. In this picture from April 4, 1975 the fishing boats break formation and head for home. A scene repeated in 55 harbours around the UK. Government assurances to the fisher's action committee were enough to persuade them to issue the codeword which ended the protest. The men had little in the way of solid promises, but they had succeeded in hammering home the message that the industry had problems needing urgent and sustained attention.

The first section of the keel of an offshore patrol vessel is laid at Hall Russell's yard in 1975. The ship for North Sea rig patrol duties was one of five on order in a contract worth £14million.

Fishing port. A long line of trawlers at Point Law at Aberdeen Harbour in 1975.

The tripod shear poles at Waterloo Quay are demolished in 1975 as an Aberdeen Harbour landmark for more than 60 years makes way for a new oil-service development.

A crumpled mass of metal is all that's left of the shear poles after they are expertly brought down early one June morning in 1975.

Hall Russell shop stewards get a send-off and a message from their workmates as they left for the Trades Union Congress in 1977. The yard was suffering from losing workers to better paid jobs in the oil industry. Workers wanted rises of up to £21 a week to staunch the flow of tradesmen out the yard gates.

Despite the huge role Aberdeen Harbour plays in the offshore oil industry there's still room to berth the little boats. With supply ships looming in the distance these weekend fishers prepare their brightly painted craft for the new season in 1977.

A bird's-eye view from February 1977 of what was about to become one of Aberdeen Harbour's busiest areas. In the centre the new P & O ferry terminal complex takes shape, getting ready for the new Shetland roll-on roll-off ferry service beginning three months later.

The new St Clair roll-on roll-off ferry ready to leave Aberdeen for Shetland and start a new era in the historic sea link with Lerwick in April 1977. The ferry loaded vehicles at the new £3million terminal at Jamieson's Quay, staying at that berth only a short time at high-water as dredging operations had not been completed.

Grampian Police piper Donald Morrison gives a traditional send-off to the latest St Clair on her maiden trip to Shetland in 1977.

A large crowd at Aberdeen Harbour to greet the Queen when she steps off the Royal Yacht *Britannia* in 1977 at the start of her Deeside holiday at Balmoral. The *Britannia* had sailed from Northern Ireland with stops at Loch Carron to see the Howard Doris Construction yard and at Scrabster to permit lunch with the Queen Mother at the Castle of Mey.

Painter Ben Collie of Stonehaven has a stunning view of Aberdeen as he works on the clock at the Harbour Board offices Regent Quay in 1975.

Supply ships loom over Aberdeen youngsters George McTavish, left, and David Cruickshank fishing off Pocra jetty, Footdee, in 1978.

Reconstruction work in full swing at Albert Quay, Aberdeen Harbour, in 1978.

An oil installation survival craft heads out of Aberdeen for sea trials in 1978.

An unusual view of Aberdeen Harbour's South Breakwater in July 1979. The picture was taken by *Evening Express* photographer Gordon Bissett.

The badly damaged Aberdeen North Pier after it took a pounding in a January 1979 storm.

Work under way to repair Aberdeen's North Pier which was damaged by heavy seas in January 1979.

In a comparatively short time after the discovery of North Sea oil Aberdeen Harbour became the most important offshore support base in Europe. This picture from 1979 shows the high level of oil related activity.

Aberdeen Harbour in 1979 showing offshore supply ships with the city beyond.

Aberdeen Harbour in 1979 with more oil industry supply ships and the North Sea in the distance.

Apprentice engineer David Anderson of Aberdeen is instructed in lathe work at Hall Russell by machining instructor Steven Pixie in 1979.

A hall Russell worker, George McLennan, carefully sets the nerve centre of the gas burner which cuts the shaped ship plates from a one-tenth scale pattern.

Joiner Raymond Morrison puts the finishing touches to a cabin in the Hall Russell yard.

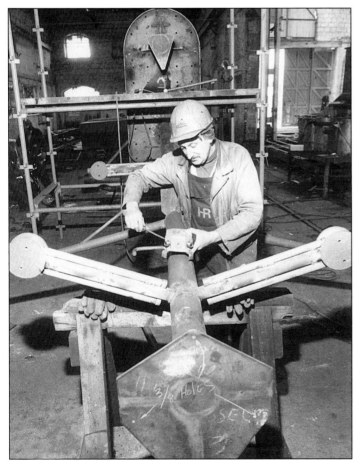

A junction box is fitted to the main mast of a Hall Russell built ship. the box will accommodate navigation lights.

Apprentice draughtsman Bill Morrison looks at some of the crests of the many vessels built at Hall Russell's Aberdeen yards over the years while Alex Barclays paints crests for the latest vessel.

Ship draughtsman Stephen Hamilton fills in some detail on a plan at Hall Russell in 1979.

Welding work on a new ship at the Hall Russell shipyard, Aberdeen, in 1979.

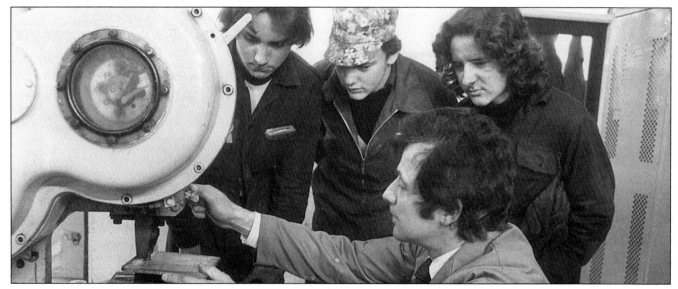

Senior instructor on fabrication Glennie Smith shows apprentice boilermakers how to punch holes in a mid steel plate in 1979. Looking on are, from left, Alex Smith, Mike Lynch and Graham Farquhar.

Harvest of the Ocean

The trawler fleet at berth in Aberdeen in 1973.

Fish being unloaded from a trawler in Aberdeen in 1974.

Reconstruction work beginning at the Palmerston Quay section of Aberdeen fish market in 1974. Thousands of tons of gravel were used to reclaim this corner of Albert Basin from the sea. Steel piling outlines where the new quay was to be built. The whole project, including a new complex with office accommodation, roof-top parking and social amenities for market workers, was scheduled for completion in 1976.

A good catch of fish at the new improved Aberdeen Fish Market in 1975.

Lord Provost Robert Lennox is shown new plastic fish boxes in 1975. They were to replace the old wooden ones which were seen as less hygienic. The new box had the same capacity as the traditional wooden trunk, and could be stagger-stacked.

Work under way in 1976 at the Market Street end of the Albert Basin where the new fish market was to rise.

Men at work in the Aberdeen Fish
Market. The year is 1977.

Hauling the plastic fish boxes at
Aberdeen Fish Market in 1977.

Shouting out the prices at Aberdeen Fish market in 1977.

Merchants make their bids for fish at Aberdeen market in 1977.

The silver harvest of the seas laid out at Aberdeen Fish Market in 1977.

The older section of Aberdeen Fish Market at Commercial Quay. This picture was taken in 1978 when that section of the market was due to be closed at the end of March.

Work under way on a new fish market at Palmerston Quay, South Market Street. The building was due for completion by the end of 1978 with a new market building on neighbouring Albert Quay as well. At this period the industry's market space was limited with a temporary building at Pacific Wharf helping to ease the problems.

The new Aberdeen fish market area at South Market Street in 1979.

Gateway to the Skies

The first Trident jet to fly to Aberdeen on a scheduled flight loads up with passengers for the return to London in 1972. The Trident replaced a Viscount which developed a fault. The Trident, which has a capacity of more than 100 passengers, could carry only 80 on the flight because the runway was not long enough to allow a takeoff with a full load. Among the passengers was Raymond Baxter. The television personality had been in the city for the Fisheries Exhibition.

An airport ready for take-off in 1973. The Dyce site prepares to expand to cope with the increasing demand for flying and Aberdeen's status as a major oil capital.

Another small piece of history at Aberdeen Airport as holidaymakers board a Caravelle jet for a charter flight to Mallorca. It was the start of north-east folk jetting off to the sun from their home airport.

An aerial picture of Aberdeen Airport in 1973 with building work under way and the BEA helicopter hanger in the centre of the picture.

A Dan-Air scheduled flight lands at Dyce in 1974.

The first of 18 separate prefabricated modules for the new arrivals hall being constructed at under-pressure Aberdeen Airport in 1974. Work was under way to connect the modules and have the new hall open within a month.

The demand for air travel at Aberdeen soared by 100 percent in two years in the early Seventies. This new terminal is providing big improvements for travellers in 1974, but was just a temporary solution for the rapidly expanding airport. A new multi-million pound terminal was planned for 1978.

A view from the south of Aberdeen Airport in 1975 showing the main runway at top right. The bases of Bristow Helicopters British Airways Helicopters are at top left. In front of that is the partially completed aircraft apron and taxiways for the new £6.5million terminal.

A bird's-eye view of Aberdeen Airport, Dyce, shows 20 aircraft on the ground in 1974. A BAC 1-11 can be seen, bottom right, to the main runway. A Piper Aztec is about to take off. The main terminal is fronted by the light aircraft apron in the centre of the picture.

Aircraft lined up at Aberdeen Airport in 1974.

The date is September 17, 1975 and it's the busiest day in the history of Aberdeen Airport. Thanks to the Offshore Europe '75 exhibition at Bridge of Don the airport had to cope with 40 scheduled jet arrivals plus large numbers of charters and small executive planes. Our picture shows private planes parked around the aprons at Dyce.

By 1975 passenger numbers at Aberdeen Airport had soared to 450,000 and the new terminal was still some years away.

The new terminal at Aberdeen Airport takes shape towards the end of 1976.

By the mid-1970s the airport at Dyce had become the site of one of the world's busiest heliports with the 'workhorses' of the offshore oil industry now a familiar sight over Aberdeen.

The Bristow heliport at Aberdeen Airport in 1976 with the early morning British Airways jet flight to London taking off in the background.

An array of executive air transport parked at Aberdeen Airport in September 1977 when the Offshore Europe exhibition attracted the world's oil industry high fliers.

The mix of jets, turbo-props and helicopters which had become a familiar sight at Aberdeen Airport by 1978.

Aberdeen's £3million terminal building is opened by Princess Alexandra in 1977 to at last give Europe's oil capital the airport it needed. The terminal was part of an £8.5million development including cargo complex, car parks, roads, new apron and taxiways. During her visit, accompanied by husband Angus Ogilvy, the Princess met Gandar Dower, the air pioneer who founded the Dyce airport in the 1930s.

A typically busy scene at Aberdeen Airport's terminal building in 1978.

Changing Face

A helicopter from the nearby heliport flies over the new industrial estate which attracting a lot of interest from oil-related companies in 1974.

The growing Kirkhill industrial estate in 1978 with a reminder in the foreground that Dyce had just recently been a rural village.

The housing complex at the Hilton Road and Rosehill Drive junction takes shape in February 1978.

A 15-storey block of flats on Rose Street just after it was completed in 1975.

Road and rail routes through Aberdeen make an intricate design in this aerial picture from 1977. The large Mounthooly roundabout dominates the centre of the picture. The roads leading on to it are (from the left), Mounthooly, Nelson Street, West North Street, Gallowgate, Hutcheon Street and Causewayend.

Cornhill Court, an example of the municipal housing which flourished in the 1970s.

(next page) An aerial picture from the mid-1970s showing the sweep of Aberdeen's Union Street with much of the city centre building of that era evident, sitting alongside the elegant buildings of earlier eras.

Parts of the old city of Aberdeen disappear in November 1971 for a new stretch of dual carriageway at East North Street. The roadway meant the disappearance of a car and lorry park in East North Street and gave a fresh look to the Park Street-Beach Boulevard-Commerce Street-Justice Street junction.

Commerce Street and the Beach Boulevard in 1977 with the Virginia and Marischal Court high flats.

The Northern Co-operative Society building, left, and the Technical College, bottom, are the buildings which dominate this picture from 1979.

Aberdeen's Anderson Drive ring road with multi-storey flats at Stockethill towering over the scene in 1977.

The north-east hospital complex at Foresterhill, Aberdeen, in the throes of building work in 1974. Today the site continues to see new and ever larger buildings springing up.

Stockethill high-rise flats rise up in 1968... shaping the new homes of the Seventies on the site of the prefabs which provided popular homes in the post-war era.

Bridge of Don industrial estate as it was in November 1975.

A new housing development at Bridge of Don on the Persley Road. The picture was taken looking east with the high flats of Seaton visible in the background. This private development of 150 homes is pictured in September 1973.

One of the first houses to be built at Bridge of Don by George Wimpey under contract for Aberdeenshire Housing Committee is officially opened by committee chairman Alex Rennie in December 1973.

A long line of new homes stretching from the core of Phase One of the Bridge of Don new town. Beyond Phase One work is just beginning on Phase Two. Eventually the 90 acres in Phase One was augmented by 250 acres in Phase Two in the area to the north of the Parkway.

Looking across the River Don towards work proceeding at the high flats on King Street just beyond the bridge.

The Upper Denburn in 1970 before the massive redevelopment of the area. The Spa Bar, a popular old pub is in the centre of the picture.

The Denburn covered car park for 600 cars taking shape in 1973 with the old infirmary building in the background.

Cranes at work as the eighth floor of the 22-storey high flats at the Upper Denburn takes shape towards the end of 1971.

It's January 1973 and a new tower block has taken its place on Aberdeen's skyline.

Denburn Court looms over the health centre in July 1974.

The Denburn Health Centre and two of its satisfied customers in 1976.

A cake model of the Denburn Health Centre is cut during the official opening in 1976. From left, convener of Grampian Region, Sandy Mutch, Lord Provost Robert Lennox, Aberdeen North MP Bob Hughes, W.S. Crosby, chairman of the Grampian Health Board, A.R. Batchelor, secretary and District Administrator J.J. Sapsworth.

The BP building rises at the Farburn site in Dyce in 1977.

A new look to Dyce in the north-east's post oil years in 1975.

Mrs Charlotte Simpson looks on as her home in Old Torry is demolished in 1974 after initially refusing to move until the council met her terms.

Lord Kirkhill officially opens the Shell UK Exploration and Production Ltd marine supply base at Torry, Aberdeen, in 1975. Looking on, from the left, are Peter Bexendell, chairman of the board of Shell UK, Mrs Lennox, Aberdeen Lord Provost Robert Lennox and Lady Kirkhill.

The Shell UK office block at Altens, Aberdeen, takes shape in 1977.

The Broad Street archaeological dig works against time to check the ancient part of the city in 1973 after the Aberdeen Journals building was demolished and before the Town House extension was built. The excavation, which also covered Queen Street, uncovered thousands of fragments and relics from medieval Aberdeen. An entire 14th-century glazed jug was found in the dig. The treasures found led historians to rethink just how old the city is. Evidence was found of habitation in that area in 6000BC, 4,000 years earlier than historians had previously believed to be the case.

The New Market in Aberdeen under construction in 1973.

Aberdeen's Model Lodging House on East North Street in 1978.

The sitting area of the Model Lodging House in 1978 when it still occupied a big site in East North Street, Aberdeen. The hostel for single working men opened in 1899 and could house 250 people. The building closed in 1988 and was converted into a block of 39 flats which won an award for their design.

One of the lodging house 'room' at East North Street when it provided shelter for many needy men.

In 1975 vandalism and litter was as big an issue as it is today. This group of angry residents at Kincorth Circle were protesting about under-age drinking and the amount of litter strewn around.

The tariffs at the Model Lodging House on Monday, November 13, 1978.

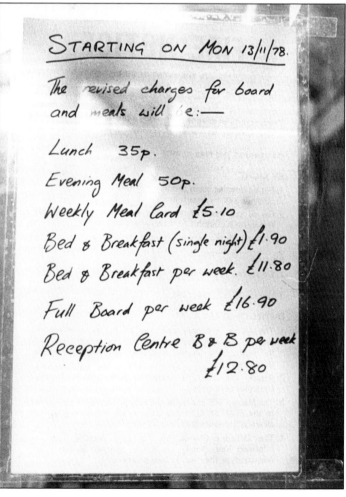

STARTING ON MON 13/11/78.

The revised charges for board and meals will be:—

Lunch   35p.

Evening Meal 50p.

Weekly Meal Card £5.10

Bed & Breakfast (single night) £1.90

Bed & Breakfast per week. £11.80

Full Board per week £16.90

Reception Centre B & B per week £12.80

By 1979 the covered car park at the Denburn Centre was undergoing tests by architects and builders. Water leakages had plagued the car park more or less from its opening. Stalactites up to six inches long appeared on the roof of the car park but a solution to the problem proved elusive.

A new roundabout at Market Street, Aberdeen, in 1974.

The site of the popular and plush Gaumont Cinema on Union Street, Aberdeen, becomes a building site in 1974.

The change in the public's leisure habits in the 1970s brought a drop in movie attendances and many cinema buildings fell empty. Here the year is 1974 and where the Majestic Cinema once stood there is a gap site.

Rose Street as it was in 1976. The West End Soda Fountain and William Scorgie, grain and potato merchants can be seen on the left. Two businesses from earlier eras.

The Aberdeen prefabricated homes from the post World War Two finally disappeared in the Seventies. Intended for only a decade or two they proved popular homes for nearly four decades. These prefabs were in Tullos.

Mastrick in 1973. Part of the large Aberdeen housing scheme in Mastrick which was home to 18,000 people.

Aberdeen adapted to high-flats living in the 1970s. This view of the 'whirlies' on the drying green area was taken from the fourteenth floor of a Mastrick Land building and provides the photographer with an intriguing picture.

The Boots shop in Aberdeen's Union Street in 1973.

Woolworths in 1979 at its long-time Union Street base,

The New Towns

The Seventies saw the growth of new towns and huge suburbs to cope with the demand for homes. Plans for those big projects often stretched into the previous decade. In the case of Westhill the private company behind a scheme for a 'town' of 8,000 went public with their plans in 1965. The news of the development came from Ronald F. Dean, an Aberdeen solicitor who had the vision of a township on a 550-acre site at Westhill, Skene. In 1965 he saw the potential of this 'poor agricultural land'. By 1972 the plans for the Westhill Garden suburb were unveiled.

Looking from Wester Kinmundy towards the area marked down for development as the Westhill garden suburb. This picture was taken in 1965 looking towards the west.

Features of the Westhill project are pointed out by developer Sidney Denman, with (on the left) Ronald Dean, and partners, architects and a councillor.

Westhill is still as much 'garden' as 'suburb' in this picture from early 1970s.

The growing township. A 1977 picture of expanding Westhill.

In 1979 the Westhill shopping centre was under construction.

The year is 1975 and Westhill Golf Course greenkeeper William Clelland is confident the first balls will be struck on the fairways in the spring of the following year. Working with Mr Clelland on the sixth tee is apprentice greenkeeper Stuart Davidson.

Westhill Academy starts to take shape in 1977.

The rapidly growing new township at Westhill pictured in 1974.

All roads lead to...
Kintore. An exercise
self-promotion from
1972.

ABERDEEN	12
ALFORD	16
BANCHORY	16
STONEHAVEN	27
MONTROSE	50
BRAEMAR	58
FORFAR	63
ARBROATH	63
DUNDEE	85
PERTH	90
STIRLING	126
EDINBURGH	134
GLASGOW	154
LANARK	161
AYR	187
PRESTWICK	182
CARLISLE	224
NEWCASTLE	240
YORK	312
LIVERPOOL	338
BIRMINGHAM	415
LONDON	540
LANDS END	686

INVERURIE	5
OLDMELDRUM	9
HUNTLY	27
KEITH	38
BANFF	39
BUCKIE	50
TOMINTOUL	55
ELGIN	56
LOSSIEMOUTH	62
KINLOSS	62
FORRES	66
GRANTOWN ON SPEY	69
AVIEMORE	74
NAIRN	78
INVERNESS	92
DINGWALL	114
INVERGORDON	119
FORT WILLIAM	158
ISLE OF SKYE	186
WICK	215
THURSO	236
DOUNREAY	241
JOHN O' GROATS	232

Just Folk

The University of Aberdeen's new rector, entertainer 'Professor' Jimmy Edwards, serves up the traditional free drinks at the Kirkgate Bar in 1973.

Politics can be a dirty business. Prominent north-east Liberals Councillor Nigel Lindsay and David Gracie, prospective Liberal candidate for West Aberdeenshire, rolled up their trousers and went for a paddle with sample bottles at the source of one of Aberdeen's most famous pongs. Unfortunately this much publicised bit of muck raking in 1973 failed to attract much public interest. Only the Press and television men turned up.

Aberdeen's new television detector van sets out in 1973 to find people who haven't an up to date licence.

On July 10, 1973 the temperature in Aberdeen reached only a very average 17.5°C (63.5°F). But that did not deter this hardy foursome on holiday from Leicester. Mr and Mrs George Glover and Mr and Mrs W. Sykes make the most of a visit to Aberdeen Beach in 1973.

Seventies fashion on display beside Aberdeen Beach Ballroom on a sunny holiday in 1973.

Splashing out at Aberdeen beach for a bracing dip in the sea in 1973.

Miss World Belinda Green meets one of the Duthie Park's Shetland ponies on March 13, 1973. The 21-year-old Australian was in Aberdeen at the invitation of the Corporation Parks and Recreation Department to plant a maple in the forecourt of the park restaurant and a sycamore tree at Union Terrace Gardens.

Tattie howkers take a break from their work in 1973 when Tattie Holidays were still a part of rural life.

I don't know what the council buses are coming to! An Outspan 'orange car' takes to Union Street on a publicity stunt in 1973.

Still learning the old skills. Workers at the Devanha cooperage, Aberdeen, in 1973.

An Olympic gold medallist in the making. David Wilkie back in Aberdeen in September 1973 with his parents. The swimmer is proudly displaying the two medals he won at the world swimming championships in Belgrade – a gold for the 200 metres breaststroke which he won in a world record time, and a bronze for the 200 metres medley. David was taking the opportunity to spend a few days with his parents before flying back to college at Miami, Florida, to continue his studies and work to swim even faster.

Aberdeen fish merchant Joe Little pictured in 1973 with his Italian supercar, a Lamborghini.

Grampian Television personality of 1973 Jim MacLeod holds aloft his trophy. Viewers voted for the veteran bandleader who was presented with the award at Grampian's Hogmanay programme.

Street photographers were once a familiar sight on Aberdeen's Union Street. This one was snapped himself in 1973.

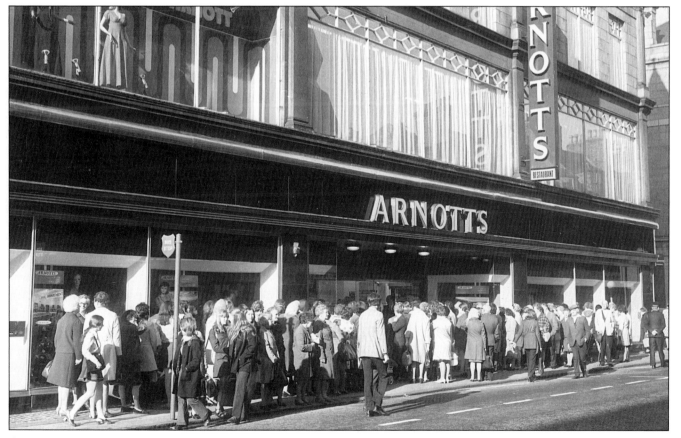

Crowds gather outside Arnotts in 1973 when Sir Hugh Fraser opened the remodelled George Street store. Sir Hugh, head of the House of Fraser, had overseen this outlet change from being Isaac Benzies to Arnotts, one of 11 such stores throughout Scotland. New to the store was a Miss Arnott Boutique, a new hairdressing salon and revamped restaurant.

The firm that was thought to be Scotland's oldest cycle shop closed down in Aberdeen in March 1973. George Bruce, the owner of Bruce's Lawn Mower Services, had decided to call it a day at the age of 68. His grandfather's firm was called Wellington Cycles when he took over new premises at Holburn Junction in 1884. The premises had previously been Babby Law's, a famous Aberdeen pub. Mr Bruce is pictured outside the shop with a penny-farthing which he restored after getting the dilapidated machine for the cost of repairing a woman's mower.

Rolf Harris does a jig in Highland dress as he celebrates Hogmanay in Aberdeen. The Australian entertainer was in the city to take part in the show *For Auld Lang Syne* at His Majesty's Theatre. The BBC broadcast the show live from the theatre as their 1974 Hogmanay special.

Television star Noele Gordon checks out the *Evening Express* programme listings with editor Robert Smith looking on in 1974.

With a General Election imminent Tory Opposition leader Edward Heath at Aberdeen Airport, Dyce, in September 1974 to begin a gruelling 15-hour tour of the north-east's Nationalist strongholds. By his side is West Aberdeenshire MP Russell Fairgrieve. Prime Minister Harold Wilson did call an election for October, which he won.

Prime Minister Harold Wilson and his wife Mary arrive at Aberdeen Airport, Dyce, on September 7, 1974. The Prime Minister was dodging the rain... and a hail of reporters questions about a General Election date. The couple were heading for Balmoral as the guest of the Queen as the Braemar Gathering got under way. And the Prime Minister was still keeping everyone guessing about the General Election date when he flew out from Aberdeen Airport on September 9 after his weekend at Balmoral.

Disc jockey Dave Fraser and some dancegoers at the Palace Ballroom, Aberdeen, in 1974.

Newspaper tycoon Lord Thomson of Fleet checks up on one of the many newspapers he owns as he waits for his plane at Aberdeen Airport, Dyce, after his first visit to an oil rig in 1974. With the Press Baron are, from left, Gordon Brunton of the Thomson Organisation Ltd, Bob McAllister, of Occidental Petroleum and his wife, and on the extreme right, Mrs Brunton.

Press baron Lord Thomson, whose family had major interests in the North Sea oil industry, waves his copy of the *Evening Express* after visiting the oil rig *Ocean Victory* in 1974. With him is Gordon Brunton, managing director of the Thomson Organisation.

Entertainer Andy Stewart and two of the cast in his 1974 show at His Majesty's Theatre, Aberdeen.

In 1974 there were horse and carriage rides for children at Aberdeen's Duthie Park.

A dog grabs the spotlight as Air Training Corps cadets prepare for a trip at Aberdeen Railway Station during the local 1974 Trades Fortnight.

Everything to play for at the start of another game at the draughts squares on Union Terrace Gardens in 1974.

Pupils at Summerhill School during a mass walk-out in April 1974 to protest at the suspension of headmaster R.F. Mackenzie by the Aberdeen Education Committee. The innovative teacher said from his home: 'I am immensely proud that the pupils feel so strongly about it that they should do this.'

Proving that llamas take a fair bucket is first footing Herbert. He is pictured making a New Year call on Aberdeen Zoo manager George Leslie at the start of 1975.

One of Aberdeen Zoo's lion cubs is the centre of attention on a flag day for the World Wildlife Fund in 1974.

Crowds are held back at Union Bridge, Aberdeen, in 1974 during a hoax bomb alert.

The skiers concentrate as they tackle the dry ski slope at Stoneywood in 1974.

Cooling down in Aberdeen on a hot summer's day in 1975.

The Westburn Park attracts crowds during the heatwave of 1975, and the pond's a favourite with the children.

Two young women, Katie Williamson and Moira McIntyre, show how they're keeping cool in the Westburn Park during the heatwave of 1975.

'Onion Johnny' Henri Chapalain shows off strings of his wares to Mrs E.M. Finlayson of the Royal Horticultural Society of Aberdeen in Aberdeen in 1975. The society wanted a genuine 'ingin Johnny for their annual September show but had great difficulty tracking down the elusive onion sellers until Henri was traced. He told Mrs Finlayson that he and his two helpers would be delighted to appear at the show.

Onions for sale. French farmer Henri Chapalain who was the third generation of his Britanny family to make annual trips to Scotland selling their crop of onions direct to the public. He said: 'I first came over with my father when I was 21. And he had previously accompanied his father to Scotland.' He said that his group of three were the only French onion sellers continuing to operate in the north-east. Using a van and the traditional onion-festooned bicycles Henri and his colleagues, operating from a base at St Peter's Lane, Aberdeen, cover an area from Arbroath to Nairn between September and New Year.

Part-time wicker-work enthusiast David Smith back at work after surviving being hit by lightning in July 1975. Mr Smith, a retired warehouseman, was in his garden shed working on a straw bee skep when the thunderstorm broke and his raised aluminium skep needle was struck by lightning. The needle was hurled across the shed and Mr Smith, of South Crown Street, Aberdeen, was left with a numb hand for a time. Following retirement Mr Smith had been busily occupied making the wicker beehives.

City dog catcher Mrs Moira Adams with some of her four-legged friends, Julie, Brandy and Sooty. Mrs Adams had run the Dogs' Wag-in shop for five years before she took up the challenge of tracking down strays in the city's council housing schemes and taking them to the dog compound at Seaton.

Aberdeen Mountain Rescue Team put on a display for the public at Dyce in 1975.

Aberdeen Music Hall was packed with 1,500 people in 1973 when opportunity knocked for local teacher Alex Green, pictured here with Hughie Green. The tin whistle player won the vote and later made an appearance on Hughie's television talent show. More than 240 acts were auditioned for the show by Hughie and his team.

Who said Rob Roy was 'armless'? Peterculter's most famous resident in 1975 after his arms were broken off as he stood overlooking the Leuchar Burn. One arm bore a shield and the other a metal sword. Locals said replacing the arms could cost £300. Within a week the missing limbs were recovered and three youths charged with theft of Rob's arms.

Four girls polish up their their act before auditions for the Hughie Green Show at the Music Hall in 1975. Television talent spotter Hughie Green auditioned 186 performers for the show which featured 12 acts. Winner on the night was Johnny Marshall, a Post Office engineer from Edinburgh, who was clapped to victory by thunderous applause from the audience.

A popular stall at the Timmer Market in Aberdeen's Castlegate in 1975.

Contestants gather together during the Miss Stonehaven event at the Royal Hotel in 1975.

The Auld Alliance is toasted in this picture taken at Aberdeen Harbour in 1975. The French sailors of the ship Le Basque give a lift to a Scots soldier.

Salmon fisher on the River Dee show off some of their day's catch in 1976.

A seed potato sale at Kittybrewster Mart in Aberdeen draws a big crowd in 1976.

Entertainer Andy Stewart holds his 14-week-old baby daughter Magdalen Jean after her Christening at Banchory Ternan East Parish Church in 1977. Looking on with Andy's wife Sheila and the Revd William Nicholson are family (from left) Andrew, Melanie, Debbie, Tara and Linsey.

Aberdeen manager Ally Macleod meets the fans at a special night in the Lang Stracht in 1977 with star striker Joe Harper looking on.

Shoppers at Frasers on Union Street in 1977.

Stonehaven open-air swimming pool in 1977 with two girls who are making the most of the good weather.

Ricki Scott entertains children at Union Terrace Gardens, Aberdeen, in 1977.

A gathering in the East Neuk, Aberdeen, to mark the death of Elvis Presley, 'The King' of rock'n'roll on August 16, 1977.

Fans choose their favourite numbers at the Elvis Presley memorial gathering in the East Neuk in 1977.

Scotland's first new Roman Catholic bishop for more than five years, Father Mario Conti, is installed in Aberdeen in 1977. Bishop Mario Conti of Aberdeen was told he must raise himself above 'the ordinary mortal' by Archbishop Thomas Winning of Glasgow, the man whom Bishop Conti was destined to succeed.

Meet the backstage VIP at His Majesty's Theatre in April 1977 – Scott Francis Gordon. His proud parents Joe Gordon and Sally Logan, the Scottish folk duo had been appearing in the Sydney Devine Show. The duo have turned down the chance of a tour of Australia to give Scott a settled start to life, but they do plan to take him on a Canadian tour next year.

Aberdeen's June Imray presents copies of her record The Torry Quine to two fans.

In 1977 David Buchan qualified as the United Kingdom's youngest pilot at just 17 years old. The Hazlehead Academy pupil breezed through an hour-long flying test to complete his training.

The performers line up for a souvenir picture at a *Good Old Days* night of entertainment at Stonehaven Town Hall in 1977.

Ready to take part in an It's A Knockout competition at Stonehaven Gala in 1977.

Close attention from possible buyers in 1977 at an Aberdeen sale of lost and found property.

Road sweepers at work in Mastrick in February 1979, making the pavements safe by spreading sand on them..

Scots entertainers Jimmy Shand and Jack Sinclair pictured in 1977.

The Chinese New Year is celebrated in the Regency Hotel, Aberdeen, in 1977.

Seaside fever? Aberdeen beach summer fun with a disco dancing competition in 1977.

Fans of the king of rock and roll leave Aberdeen in 1979 for an Elvis Presley event in 1979.

A group of Summerhill Centre members prepare for the 1979 Aberdeen Festival Parade.

Boris the giant teddy takes the fancy of little Scott Laddiman of Milltimber. Boris was used to help raise cash for the Scottish Children's league of the RSSPCC when he was a prize at the Snow Ball at Aberdeen Beach Ballroom.

A delegation of angry Aberdeen tenants pictured in 1979 with a list of the 60 houses they claim are damp. The list was presented to the District Council's director of law and administration.

Models show off their outrageous clothes at Aberdeen's first punk show in October 1979. The style which shocked so many people in the Seventies was being used here to raise money for underprivileged children. Organiser of the evening at the Music Hall was Mrs Rose Haston of the city's punk rock shop Slaughter in King Street. Punk style wasn't just on the stage. As the latest records pulsated across the hall the audience showed off their own takes on punk style and punk dancing.

Getting About

Bus drivers and conductresses at Alexander and Sons were given a new-look in May 1970. Smart lightweight suits and modern styling replaced the heavyweight suits of old. The conductress is Heather Redman and the conductor John Gordon.

Mechanical conductors in 1971. Preparing for the new machines which allow passengers to purchase their own tickets.

A new-style bus goes on show outside His Majesty's Theatre, Aberdeen, in 1973.

The Aberdeen Station as it looked for many years with its distinctive departure and arrivals windows, newsagent and the artillery shells which collected money for the YMCA. On this occasion in 1973 the station is deserted due to a rail dispute which caused all trains to be cancelled.

The start of a new bus service from Aberdeen to London in 1973.

Buses pull up beside cars parked on Union Street in December 1973, long before bus lanes were thought of.

The growth of travelling abroad continued apace in the 1970s. This group on a trip organised by the *Evening Express* are heading for Holland in 1979.

A Scatterburn bus on its way to Shetland in 1979! The Aberdeen bus is on the deck of the Northern Isles ferry *St Magnus*. It was being transported long-established Lerwick town service of John Leask and Son.

Thank You for the Music

Glam-rock group The Sweet with singer Brian Connolly up front gets a frenzied response from the fans at a concert in Aberdeen's Beach Ballroom. The group were on a troubled five-day tour of Scotland in 1973. The four-man group's camp clothes and make-up had attracted a lot of adverse comment. Their Kilmarnock gig, just before they played in Aberdeen, was stopped in a hail of bottles and eggs coming from one section of the crowd.

Dave Cousins, the driving force behind the popular group the Strawbs in full flow at an Aberdeen concert in 1973.

Robert Plant of Led Zeppelin at a memorable sell-out concert by the supergroup in 1973 at the Music Hall, Aberdeen.

Singer Robert Plant and the master guitarist Jimmy Page entertain an Aberdeen audience in 1973. Helping provide the big sound at the Music Hall were other Led Zeppelin members John Bonham and John Paul Jones.

David Bowie in Ziggy Stardust guise tries to win over a rather sceptical Aberdeen audience at the Music Hall in 1973.

Scots singer Lulu autographs a football for Aberdeen football team Middlefield Wasps in 1973 with well-known city publican Harold Bell on the left.

The New Seekers take a bow at the Music Hall, Aberdeen, in 1974. They are (from left), Paul Layton, Eve Graham, Marty Kristian, Lyn Paul and Peter Oliver.

Plaid again ...the Bay City Rollers in their tartan-trimmed outfits at Aberdeen in 1974.

Scream it again ...a fan let's her feelings be known at a Bay City Rollers concert at the Capitol Cinema in 1975. An attendant looks on in amazement.

It just needed a rumour of the arrival of their heroes to bring out the Bay City Rollers' fans in 1975. This group – like another 100 youngsters – turned up at Aberdeen Airport to greet the group ...but they weren't there.

A sea of tartan and Bay City Rollers' scarves at the Capitol Cinema in 1974.

Shouting out for the Bay City Rollers in Aberdeen in 1974.

A surge of enthusiasm from fans of the Bay City Rollers is kept under control by policemen at a queue outside the Capitol Cinema, Union Street, Aberdeen, for tickets in 1975.

An attendant stops a fan rushing the stage during a 1975 Bay City Rollers concert in Aberdeen.

A fan is removed from the stage during the David Essex concert at the Capitol in 1977.

Standing ovation for David Essex from his fans in Aberdeen in 1977.

David Essex on song during a 1975 visit to Aberdeen.

A typical David Essex pose during a 1975 concert at the Capitol, Aberdeen.

Cliff Richard has been a visitor to Aberdeen throughout his long career. Here the clean-cut singer is seen during a Gospel singing performance at the Music Hall in 1974 – his first visit to the city in 15 years. Capacity audiences at the Music Hall heard two concerts reflecting the singer's Christian beliefs.

Six Cliff Richard fans meet their hero courtesy of an *Evening Express* competition. They all attended Cliff's show at the Capitol Cinema, Aberdeen, in November 1975 before having a chat with the star afterwards.

Cliff Richard gets a double kiss from two of his most travelled fans during a visit to Aberdeen in 1978. Tokio girls Toshiko Uchioike and Kyoko Hamada were in Europe for seven weeks and made sure they were in Britain at the time of Cliff's tour. They attended all seven of his Gospel concerts, including the tour finale at the Music Hall, Aberdeen.

Pop star Tommy Steels and England batsman Mike Denness have some fun after meeting up at Aberdeen Airport in September 1976 when the London plane arrived. Tommy was in the city to arrange a show at His Majesty's Theatre and the Denness, a former England cricket team skipper, was heading to Fochabers for a coaching week and charity matches. Looking on are Mike's lifelong friend Gordon Baxter, of Baxter's of Speyside and James Donald of His Majesty's Theatre.

Entertainer Tommy Steele high-stepping through rehearsals at Aberdeen's His Majesty's Theatre in November 1976, with some of the cast of his Anniversary Show.

Medallion man. Neil Sedaka performing at the Capitol, Aberdeen, in 1975.

Recording star Neil Sedaka signs copies of his album Overnight Success for two Aberdeen fans in 1975.

Popular Aberdeen pop group Superklute pictured in 1977.

Prince Charles and The Three Degrees share a joke backstage at His Majesty's Theatre in 1978. The US group had been performing at a charity show in aid of the Prince's Trust. Sheila, Helen and Valerie broke into giggles and laughter when the kilted Prince surveyed their slinky black dance suits and said: 'You're wearing trousers tonight and I'm wearing the skirt.' Other stars at the Royal Gala show were comedian and ex-Goon Michael Bentine, magician Paul Daniels, singer Peter Morrison and ventriloquist Roger de Courcey.

Artworld

The chorus of the Lyric Musical Society bring lamps into action when they had to keep two steps ahead of power-cut blackouts during the fuel crisis of February 1972. The society were determined not to lose any rehearsal time for their production of *Hello Dolly*, even if the lights went out. Their show-must-go-on determination was shown when fuel conservation began and they lost their rehearsal room at Beechwood School. They moved to Powis Academy hall until the Corporation moved to stop all school use for recreational purposes. But the Lyric weren't going to be denied rehearsal time and moved to His Majesty's Theatre rehearsal rooms in Union Terrace.

Kenny Ball and his Jazzmen fool around at the Royal Darroch in 1975 when they arrived in the North-east on one of the highly popular tours by the traditional jazz band.

North-east clothes designer Bill Gibb and a model wearing one of his creations at Grampian Television studios in 1975.

The stars of the Alexander Brothers Show enjoying themselves in Union Terrace Gardens, Aberdeen. The Brothers' show was a popular summer event at His Majesty's Theatre in the Seventies.

Practical art. In 1976 a new feature at Aberdeen Art Gallery was this Perspex cylinder which looked good and was also a collecting box for the Friends of Aberdeen Art Gallery and Museum.

The final dramatic scene from *Orpheus In The Underworld* which was staged at the Arts Centre by Aberdeen Opera Company in 1976.

The can-can dancers kicking out during the 1976 Aberdeen Opera Company production of *Orpheus In The Underworld*.

A visitor to Aberdeen Art Gallery listens to a cassette recorder describing a fibreglass sculpture. Three young people on the Government Job Creation Scheme researched information about the works in the gallery and wrote scripts for the audio aids for visitors.

If it wisnae for your wellies... comedian Billy Connolly recalls one of his comic songs as he hams it up during a visit to Aberdeen in 1979.

A bit of fun at a rehearsal for *The Mikado* in 1979. Aberdeen Opera Company musical director Arthur Bruce makes a point to pianist Lynda Reid.

Visitors to Aberdeen Art Gallery are attracted by an exhibit of hand hooked tapestry by Alan Davie in 1978.

Aberdeen Opera Company going through their paces in their production Trilogy 78. On the left is Barry Fenwick with Brian McDonald and Evelyn Smith.

Smiling Through

A scene from 1970 which shows that though the weather in the North-east can be fierce, it can also be beautiful. The weak January sun's rays are reflected on an ice-covered River Dee with the old Bridge of Dee in the distance.

The awesome power of the sea is captured in this study of waves crashing over Aberdeen Harbour's South Breakwater in 1972.

The year is 1972 and these two ladies at Aberdeen Royal Infirmary Porters and Maids supper dance at the White Cockade, Aberdeen, are enjoying their meal despite a power cut. Striking miners' blockades of power stations had resulted in compulsory cuts. Newspapers carried the times of the cuts in the various areas of the city. Thousands of workers in Aberdeen bore the brunt of the disruption as they tried to keep the wheels of industry turning.

Publican Harry Nicoll of the Four Mile House, Bucksburn, beats the blackout with his own version of personal lighting in 1972. Two torch bulbs attached to the legs of his spectacles are powered by a battery in his jacket pocket. The system was devised by a customer, Henry Lees of Bucksburn.

Darkened Union Street in February 1972 after the power cuts blacked out Aberdeen's shop lights.

The Rosemount area of Aberdeen is blacked out but fish and chip lovers get their favourite dish served by the light of a gas lamp.

In 1973 when workmen were building the Sheraton Hotel at Bucksburn (now the Britannia Hotel) a torrent and flood swept through the site upending a 25-ton excavator.

The torrential rain in December 1973 also caused a burn to burst its banks and make an island of these cottages on the Swailend road near Newmachar. The wild month of December brought a 24-hour non-stop torrent of rain followed by blizzards. Hundreds of acres of farming land was flooded by rivers which burst their banks. Farmers trying to assess the damage were hampered by a dense fog which reduced visibility almost to nil.

When the snow came in 1973 these Aberdeen skiing enthusiasts grabbed the opportunity to take to the Garhdee slopes.

Aberdeen Zoo called on all hands to clear the snow in 1973.

The white stuff... the Pittodrie area, and the Dons' stadium, under a covering of snow in 1973.

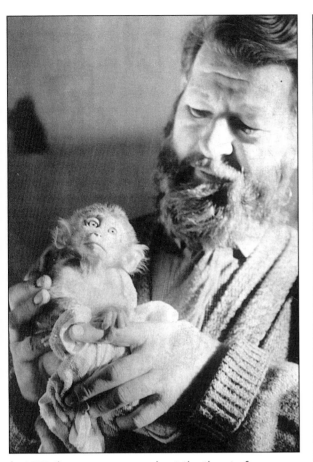

In 1970 there was concern about the threat of power cuts. Manager George Leslie said an electricity cut could cause the deaths of monkeys, snakes and fish. He is holding Brenda, a pig-tail Macaque which was abandoned by her mother and can only survive with a powerful heating light shining on her cage all the time.

A rueful smile from farmer's wife Mrs Brenda Minty, pictured amid the remains of a 30ft Dutch barn and cattle court after a storm swept through Crossley Farm in February 1974.

Holiday Monday weather in Aberdeen in 1975.

The scene at the junction of Aberdeen's Forest Avenue and Union Grove in September 1976 after gale-force winds battered the city.

More havoc caused by the September gale in 1976. A giant seafront exhibition lies flattened at Queen's Links, Aberdeen. Thirty workmen were preparing the tent for the international fisheries exhibition Catch '76 when it collapsed and seven were injured. Terrified workers ran for their lives dodging tons of thrashing canvas, flying metal poles and fittings and equipment being blown around 'like matchwood'. One eyewitness said: 'The whole top blew off. Tent poles and stands collapsed and all the people inside were being blown across the floor.'

Another uprooted tree in Aberdeen after the gale of 1976. This tree lies on a house at the premises of W. Smith and Son Ltd at Hazledene Road.

After the storm. A tree lies across the car park at Woodhill House, Aberdeen, in 1977.

A snowplough battles to free a stranded bus from snow drifts on the A9 in 1978.

A rescue helicopter lands on the main Inverness to Perth road to investigate a vehicle at the end of the railway bridge in January 1978.

Deep snow hampers rescuers on January 30, 1978 as they set out to search for four missing boy soldiers. The privates, based at York, were on their way back to Rothiemurchus after attending a dance in Aviemore when they took a shortcut and got lost in a snow storm. The boys, who sheltered overnight in a small wood, were found safe by a search party and flown by helicopter to Raigmore Hospital, Inverness.

The Ythan bursts its banks at Ellon in February 1978.

Flooding at Kintore after the downpour of February 1978.

Gordon Smith tries to keep warm in the snow after his milk float developed an electrical fault in Aberdeen's Summerhill area in January 1979.

Still managing to smile despite the weather. Tea time at an Aberdeen bus stop during a snow storm in 1979.

How do we get across to school? Flood water on Esslemont Avenue beside Aberdeen Grammar School in October 1979.

Royal Jubilee

The Queen celebrated her Silver Jubilee in 1977 and the people of Aberdeen – and the sun – came out to welcome her when she visited the city in May of that year.

One of the first groups to greet the Queen on her Silver Jubilee visit to the Silver City were these Mrs Mopps at the railway station who had a grandstand view of her arrival.

Union Street was a sea of flags and smiling faces and the crowds gathered early to get a good vantage point.

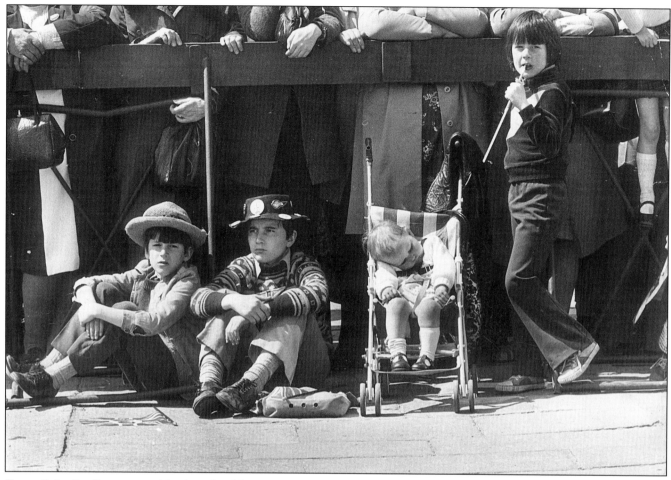

The wait for the Queen proved too long for this youngster.

A sunshine walkabout by the Queen in Broad Street ensured that for many of the people in the crowd it was a day to remember.
The impressive backdrop of Marischal College added grandeur to the scene.

One four-year-old makes sure she doesn't miss anything by perching on her mother's shoulders.

Plenty of smiling faces at this Jubilee street party at Rutherford Folds, Inverurie.

A royal word for one particular group of flag-wavers outside St Nicholas House, Broad Street.

The Queen and Duke of Edinburgh pause at the front door of the new Town House extension with the reflection of St Nicholas House caught in the smoked-glass front of the building.

The Queen waves to the crowds celebrating her Silver Jubilee as a piper adds a Scottish touch on her visit to Aberdeen.

Everyone should have one... a commemorative Silver Jubilee cup – bought by their thousands that year.

Days of Drama

A picture taken by a Russian sailor captures the moment when the *Duchess of Kent* lifeboat capsized. The *Opal* is in the foreground.

The new decade was only weeks old when terrible tragedy struck. Five Fraserburgh lifeboatmen perished when their lifeboat, *Duchess of Kent,* capsized on a mercy mission on January 21, 1970.

Remarkably one of the crew, John Jackson Brown, survived in the storm-tossed seas and was picked up by a Russian vessel. The lost men were coxswain John Stephen, chief mechanic Fred Kirkness, William Hadden, James Buchan, John Buchan and and Slessor Buchan.

The mission to help the sinking vessel the *Opal* of Skagen was to have been one of the last undertaken by the *Duchess of Kent* which was due to be replaced by a more up to date lifeboat.

The Danish fishing boat the *Opal* was under tow by a Russian vessel and being escorted by the lifeboat when she capsized.

Once again the North Sea had exacted the highest price. Just 17 years earlier six of the seven men aboard the lifeboat John and Charles Kennedy perished when it capsized at the entrance to Fraserburgh Harbour.

Within a week the Duke of Kent lead the nation's homage to the lost men as headed the thousands of mourners who followed the coffins to the Old Parish Church, Fraserburgh.

In the church four coffins lay side by side draped in the RNLI flag. One space was left in memory of Fred Kirkness whose body had not been recovered. There rested his uniform cap and an RNLI bronze medal for valour he gained in 1959.

The end of a sad mission for the Buckie lifeboat as she brings home sole survivor John Jackson Brown and the bodies of his comrades.

The Duke of Kent heads the mourners as they walk down Broad Street, Fraserburgh.

The people of Fraserburgh stand silent in respect for the lost men as the coffins and two lorries loaded with wreaths pass by.

Two firemen take a hose up to the roof of the 22, Club, Adelphi, Aberdeen, during a spectacular blaze in January 1970. The firemen were battling to prevent the blaze spreading to adjoining buildings.

Tragedy struck when a Polish trawler ran aground at Murcar Sands on January 4, 1974, in a storm so bad Aberdeen Harbour had been forced to close. Despite an heroic rescue operation three fishers perished. A Russian sailor on a tug also died in an attempt to save the stranded Poles. In all 25 Polish and nine Russian men survived, nine of them scrambled ashore unaided and made for Murcar Golf Clubhouse. The dramatic scene at Murcar as coastguards prepare to fire a line out to the grounded Nurzec.

Calm following the storm. A day after the deadly drama it's hard to imagine how men could have perished. Sightseers at Murcar look out to the trawler just a few yards off shore.

Survivors of the trawler *Nurzec* visited the tug *Gordiy* to pay a final tribute to the Russian crewman who died trying to save them. Soon afterwards the tug set sail for Riga.

A simple ceremony at Point Law for three Polish fishermen who lost their lives when the *Nurzec* ran aground. More than 100 people witnessed the service aboard the Polish trawler Rudawa before it left for home with its sad cargo.

The crew of the *Ben Gulvain* were winched to safety at the end of January 1976, after the top-grossing trawler ran aground at Balgownie. Coastguards fired lines out to the ship and a helicopter flew backwards for half a mile in near gale-force conditions to get a line from an oil supply ship on the stranded trawler. But rough seas foiled that first bid to free the *Ben Gulvain*.

The 17-man crew were airlifted to safety then went back on board again as the weather improved. They managed to free the trawler with the help of a tug and another trawler only to face another airlift 24 hours later when the *Ben Gulvain* was driven ashore a mile further north. Other hazardous attempts to free the ship failed before a group of Peterhead men managed to get her refloated two months after she ran aground and initially took the ship to North Queensferry.

An anxious moment as a crewman is winched off the stranded *Ben Gulvain*. Other members of the crew can be seen at the prow of the vessel.

A second attempt to haul the *Ben Gulvain* off the sand fails after the tow line snaps.

Yet another ship ashore on Aberdeen's beaches in 1976. This is the Leith trawler *Karemma* which ran aground in gale-force conditions on March 12, 1976. This time there were no casualties. The hopelessly grounded *Kareema* is pictured half-a-mile south of the Don estuary.

Fishers help gather the gear washed ashore from the stricken *Kareema*.

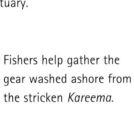

The glove factory blaze in September 1977 was one of the fiercest and most spectacular Aberdeen had seen for many years.

Neighbours in Rose Street could feel the searing heat as firemen fought to control the blazing Harrott factory In 1977. At the height of the blaze residents in the nearby Thistle Court multi-storey block had to be evacuated as windows cracked from the searing heat. Within a year the firm had moved into new premises. In 1990 Harrotts was sold to an Edinburgh businessman.

Firemen fight to stop flames spreading to fuel storage tanks holding 3,000 gallons. Householders close to the Turriff Service Station were evacuated and traffic was stopped and diverted as firemen tackled the blazing building. Fortunately wind gusting in the right direction helped the firemen stop the flames reaching the forecourt of the garage.

Flames shoot from the roof of the nurses' home at the Royal Aberdeen Children's Hospital during a blaze on June 18, 1979, that laid a huge pall of thick smoke over the scene. Nurses, some still in nightclothes, had to be led to safety from the building. Some had been asleep after night shifts when the fire broke out.

An aerial view of the massive blaze that ripped through the nurses' home at Aberdeen's main hospital. Firemaster Douglas Close said at the time that the fire broke out immediately above some external scaffolding on which painters had been working.

There was real drama at Pittodrie on February 6, 1971, when fire broke out in the main stand. Seven units of Aberdeen Fire Brigade fought the blaze which left a third of the stand a charred ruin. But the big headlines were about the rescue of a very special piece of silverware. The Dons were then holders of the Scottish Cup having beaten Celtic 3-1 in the Final the previous April. Firemaster John Donnachie, a Dons fan, knew the layout of the Pittodrie building and successfully directed the rescue operation. And it was Firemaster Donnachie who accepted the famous cup as it was passed to safety through the boardroom window. Eventually a young man was arrested for breaking into the stadium and setting fire to papers in the stand.

Dons players, from left, Jim Hermiston, Andy Geoghegan, Arthur Graham and Tommy McMillan view the damage to the stand at Pittodrie when they reported for training.

The damage to the stand at Pittodrie becomes clear in daylight.

Dons' chairman Dick Donald looks sadly at the fire damaged stand at Pittodrie.

The Scottish Cup is passed out of the boardroom into the safe hands of Firemaster John Donnachie when Pittodrie was ablaze in 1971.

People at Play

What's your bet? Racing types at Insch, Aberdeenshire, in 1977. Bookmaker George Kemp, left, has his satchel open as he calls the odds at the Insch Horse and Pony Association's two-day race meeting at Inschfield Farm in August 1977.

The Dons leave Aberdeen for a short end-of-season trip to Yugoslavia with manager Ally Macleod in 1977. The trip was blighted by cancelled flights and terrible weather. But the main talking point was persistent rumours – to be proved accurate before the end of the month – that Ally was about to become the Scotland team manager. Other significant events at that time was Joe Harper finishing Scotland's top scorer with 28 goals in his first full season back with Aberdeen., and the Dalry Thistle goalkeeper being provisionally signed by the Dons and called into the squad. Jim Leighton was cover for 'keeper Ally MacLean who had broken a finger.

Dons fans keeping cheerful despite the cold as they queue for tickets for a Scottish League match against Celtic in 1979. The game was postponed.

Another study of patient Dons' fans in queues to get tickets for one of their heroes' games. This picture was taken in 1973.

A study of the Dons' Hungarian maestro Zoltan Varga from 1973. Although he played for only one season, the Hertha Berlin player, who arrived at Pittodrie under the shadow of a bribery scandal, is still fondly remembered among fans for his exquisite skill as a ball player.

Dons' ace striker Joe Harper with the European Bronze Boot he won for his goal scoring exploits in the season 1971–72. This picture of Joe, with daughters Laura and Joanna, was taken in 1979 when he had scored 15 goals in 20 games and stood an outside chance of another European award.

Three promising young Aberdeen stars celebrate being capped for Scotland in 1979. Stuart Kennedy seems confident he is in safe hands as Jim Leighton and Alex McLeish hold him. Scotland manager Jock Stein picked Kennedy for the main team pool for a European Championship match against Belgium at Hampden. Leighton and McLeish played for the Under-21s.

Aberdonian footballing superstar Denis Law is shown some ball skills in 1974. The Scotland player was making some Sheddocksley Rovers players very happy. The 1973 Champion Street winners had hoped to meet Denis at a gala night to be presented with the trophy named after him, but international duties kept him away. In 1974 the Manchester City player made up for that disappointment on a quick visit to his native city when he at last met up with the Sheddocksley Rovers players.

England legend Gordon Banks, centre right, with some of the Under-23 squad he helped to coach after they arrived at Aberdeen Airport in 1974.

Don Revie, the England manager, stays in the background as assistant manager Les Cocker directs the Under-23 players during a training session at the Lads' Club playing fields at Woodside in 1974. The December friendly against Scotland at Pittodrie ended in an easy 3-0 win for the visitors. Willie Miller and Arthur Graham of the Dons featured in Willie Ormond's team.

Six youngsters who flew to London to represent Scotland in the Great Britain Safe Cycling and Moped Riding Competition in 1979. They were taking a break from going through their paces under the watchful eye of Grampian Police road safety officer Sgt Haswell Rae, right, to be presented with a trophy from Bill Tait of the Royal Society for the Prevention of Accidents. Lindsay Hood is receiving the trophy while looking on are Doug Hunter, Grampian Police; Gary Young; Stephen Bone; Sheila Graham; Aonghus Pirie and Andrew Telfer.

Youngsters improving their cycling skills by negotiating obstacles at Aberdeen in 1979.

Young Nicolas Jackson from Maidstone, Kent, finds out just how heavy the hammer is at the Ballater Highland Games in 1979. Ready to take on the challenge of hurling the hammer are Murray Brown, left, of Aboyne, and Alex Thomson of Alford.

Proud owners show off their model racing cars in Aberdeen in 1979. They are all members of the Aberdeen Radio Car Club who had just competed in their first national event. The club gained instant respect by winning the sports GT event and coming fourth in the Formula 1 race. In 1979 the cars could cost up to £250 each, reach 80mph and accelerate to 60mph in under three seconds. Posing with the cars and trophies are, from left back row, Graeme Cattanach, Allan Wilson, Graeme Murray. Front, Charles Thomson, George Sellar and Eric Bridger.

Aberdeen table tennis stars ready to journey to Cleveland near Middlesbrough to compete for Scotland in a schools international against England in 1975. The players are, from left, John Moir, Michael Stuart, Margaret Dunbar, Alan Matthew, Caroline Byres, Lesley Lawrence, Maureen Thomson, Wendy Smith, Michael Aitken, Alistair Davidson and Philip Matthew.

The Greyfriars Church Girl Guides at a camp in 1975 which had a Common Market theme. The 61st Aberdeen Guide Company are at a weekend training camp at Templars Park, Maryculter, where the 50 Guides were given talks by the police, Red Cross and mountain rescue team members.

Everyone pays attention as Constable Haswell Rae explains about cycling safety to pupils at Springhill School in 1973.

A helping lift from a helicopter as a ski tow stanchion is flown in to the Lecht ski centre in 1977.

Head greenkeeper at Hazlehead Gold Club Sandy Pirie examines a new-style grass cutter in 1973. The 'triple greens mower' meant that instead of two men spending 14 hours cutting greens, one could do it in four hours.

Entertainer Andy Stewart finds himself bunkered at the Andy Stewart pro-am at Banchory in September 1974. He gets a little help from playing partners musician Alex Sutherland and Banchory professional golfer Douglas Smart.

Work begins on a new clubhouse for Bachory Golf Club in 1979 on the site of the old clubhouse destroyed by fire the previous year. The club had been operating from temporary accommodation in the club car park since the blaze in April 1978.

Confident waves from the young cyclists taking their proficiency tests at the Beacon Community Centre, Aberdeen, in 1972.

Cups of Cheer

In 1970 Aberdeen FC met Jock Stein's mighty Celtic at Hampden in the Scottish Cup Final. The underdogs from the north, far from being overawed by the 108,434 crowd, emerged 3-1 victors. It was to be the first of three Cup Final victories the Dons' scored over Celtic in the 1970s. Aberdeen had not won a significant trophy since their League Cup win over St Mirren in 1955.

Young Dons' fans before they left by bus to cheer on their heroes during the successful 1970 Scottish Cup campaign.

Joe Harper scores from the penalty spot in the Scottish Cup Final on April 11, 1970.

Cup-tie McKay scores the late clincher which gave Aberdeen a 3-1 victory over Celtic, and the Scottish Cup. Derek Mckay also scored the winning goals in the quarter-final and semi-final in the Dons' 1969–70 Cup campaign.

Aberdeen FC captain Martin Buchan holds aloft the Scottish Cup for the fans at Hampden.

Manager Eddie Turnbull celebrates the cup victory with players and officials. On the right is the Dons' chairman Dick Donald.

Home are the heroes. Joe Harper holds up the Scottish Cup as fans clamour to see the trophy as it is paraded down Union Street.

In 1971 Aberdeen met Celtic in the Drybrough Cup Final, and once again the Dons' beat Celtic to take the silverware. Joe Harper scored from the penalty spot as Jimmy Bonthrone's team won 2-1 at Pittodrie. Dave Robb was the Dons' other scorer.

Joe Harper blasts home the Drybrough Cup winner in 1971. Celtic goalkeeper Evan Williams gets a hand to the ball but fails to stop it.

Dons' 'keeper Bobby Clark looks on bemused by a premature pitch invasion by young fans just before the final whistle during the Drybrough Cup Final.

Parading the Drybrough Cup at Pittodrie in 1971. The fans get a close-up view of the trophy at a friendly match. Their favourites beat Newcastle United 3-2 on the night.

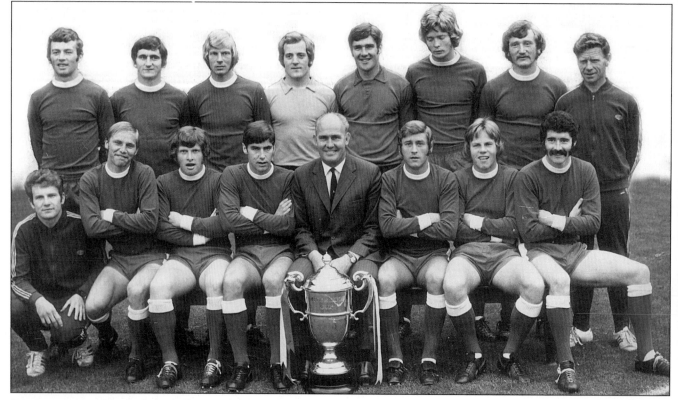

Bonthrone's boys. The Drybrough Cup-winning team. Back row (left to right): Tommy McMillan, Jim Hermiston, Henning Boel, Andy Geoghegan, Bobby Clark, Willie Young, Dave Robb and trainer Teddy Scott. Front: Ronnie Coutts (physiotherapist), George Buchan, Joe Harper, Martin Buchan, Jimmy Bonthrone, Alex Willoughby, Arthur Graham and Steve Murray.

For the second time in his still young career Dons' skipper Martin Buchan holds aloft a cup after victory over Celtic.

In 1976 the Dons won the Scottish League Cup in a dramatic Final against Celtic which wasn't settled until the second minute of extra-time when substitute Dave Robb forced home the winner. The teams finished normal time locked at 1-1 after Drew Jarvie, who conceded a penalty for Celtic's goal, headed the Dons back on level terms.

A jubilant Drew Jarvie turns to receive the acclaim of the fans after his equaliser. Earlier he had pushed Kenny Dalglish for a Celtic penalty which put them into the lead.

Dons' manager Ally MacLeod gives his team a pep talk as they head into extra-time in the League Cup Final.

Cup winner! Dave Robb puts the ball past Celtic keeper Peter Latchford to beat the Glasgow side 2-1.

The Dons' players soak up that winning feeling after beating Celtic in the 1976 League Cup Final.

Arthur Graham shows the League Cup to waiting Dons' fans outside Hampden Park after the Final, with Jocky Scott, Stuart Kennedy and Ian Fleming celebrating alongside him.

The clothes are very 1970s but that winning feeling is timeless. The Dons with their silverware.

Great scenes of jubilation as Aberdeen's fans crowd outside the Town House to see the League Cup.

Super striker Joe Harper shows the League Cup to the fans at Pittodrie which threw its gates open for the celebrations.

Pitch invasion! A sea of friendly faces at Pittodrie during the League Cup victory celebrations of 1976.

A young admirer gets a close-up of the League Cup courtesy of Joe Harper.

Goal hero Dave Robb holds the League Cup aloft for the cheering fans.

The Dons line up to acknowledge the cheers of more than 25,000 fans for their League Cup heroics. From left, Ian Fleming, Chic McLelland, Stuart Kennedy, George Campbell, Joe Harper, Drew Jarvie, Ally Maclean, Jocky Scott, Joe Smith, Arthur Graham, and (far right), Willie Garner.